FREAKY PHENOMENA

PSYCHIC ABILITIES

The Series

CONSCIOUSNESS
FAITH
HEALING
LIFE AFTER DEATH
MYSTERIOUS PLACES
PERSONALITY
PSYCHIC ABILITIES
THE SENSES

FREAKY PHENOMENA

PSYCHIC ABILITIES

Michael Centore

Foreword by Joe Nickell, Senior Research Fellow, Committee for Skeptical Inquiry

MASON CREST

Mason Crest
450 Parkway Drive, Suite D Broomall, PA 19008
www.masoncrest.com

Printed in the United States of America

First printing
9 8 7 6 5 4 3 2 1

Series ISBN: 978-1-4222-3772-4
Hardcover ISBN: 978-1-4222-3779-3
ebook ISBN: 978-1-4222-8013-3

Cataloging-in-Publication Data is available on file at the Library of Congress.

Developed and Produced by Print Matters Productions, Inc. (www.printmattersinc.com)
Cover and Interior Design by: Bill Madrid, Madrid Design
Composition by Carling Design

Picture credits: 9, Kheng Guan Toh/Shutterstock; 10, Anatoleya/iStock; 12, Beeldbewerking/iStock; 13, Renphoto/iStock; 14, dragon_fang/iStock; 16, AzmanJaka/iStock; 18-19, Sergey Nivens/Shutterstock; 20, tbradford/iStock; 22, loskutnikov/iStock; 24, sylv1rob1/Shutterstock; 25, VECTORKWORKS_ENTERPRISE/Shutterstock; 26, fotografixx/iStock; 27, jgroup/iStock; 28, RichVintage/iStock; 30, nullplus/iStock; 32, MarkCoffeyPhoto/iStock; 33, gnagel/iStock; 35, pictore/iStock; 36, molloykeith/iStock; 38, sezer66/Shutterstock; 40, Nikki Zalewski/Shutterstock; 41, sdominick/iStock; 42, iStock; 43, Wikimedia Commons

Cover: Arman Zhenikeyev/Shutterstock

CONTENTS

KEY ICONS TO LOOK FOR:

Words to understand: These words with their easy-to-understand definitions will increase the reader's understanding of the text while building vocabulary skills.

Sidebars: This boxed material within the main text allows readers to build knowledge, gain insights, explore possibilities, and broaden their perspectives by weaving together additional information to provide realistic and holistic perspectives.

Educational Videos: Readers can view videos by scanning our QR codes, providing them with additional educational content to supplement the text. Examples include news coverage, moments in history, speeches, iconic sports moments and much more!

Series glossary of key terms: This back-of-the book glossary contains terminology used throughout this series. Words found here increase the reader's ability to read and comprehend higher-level books and articles in this field.

Advice From a Full-Time Professional Investigator of Strange Mysteries

I wish I'd had books like this when I was young. Like other boys and girls, I was intrigued by ghosts, monsters, and other freaky things. I grew up to become a stage magician and private detective, as well as (among other things) a literary and folklore scholar and a forensic-science writer. By 1995, I was using my varied background as the world's only full-time professional investigator of strange mysteries.

As I travel around the world, lured by its enigmas, I avoid both uncritical belief and outright dismissal. I insist mysteries should be *investigated* with the intent of solving them. That requires *critical thinking*, which begins by asking useful questions. I share three such questions here, applied to brief cases from my own files:

Is a particular story really true?

Consider Louisiana's Myrtles Plantation, supposedly haunted by the ghost of a murderous slave, Chloe. We are told that, as revenge against a cruel master, she poisoned three members of his family. Phenomena that ghost hunters attributed to her spirit included a mysteriously swinging door and unexplained banging noises.

The Discovery TV Channel arranged for me to spend a night there alone. I learned from the local historical society that Chloe never existed and her three alleged victims actually died in a yellow fever epidemic. I prowled the house, discovering that the spooky door was simply hung off center, and that banging noises were easily explained by a loose shutter.

Does a claim involve unnecessary assumptions?

In Flatwoods, WV, in 1952, some boys saw a fiery UFO streak across the evening sky and apparently land on a hill. They went looking for it, joined by others. A flashlight soon revealed a tall creature with shining eyes and a face shaped like the ace of spades. Suddenly, it swooped at them with "terrible claws," making a high-pitched hissing sound. The witnesses fled for their lives.

Half a century later, I talked with elderly residents, examined old newspaper accounts, and did other research. I learned the UFO had been a meteor. Descriptions of the creature almost perfectly matched a barn owl—seemingly tall because it had perched on a tree limb. In contrast, numerous incredible assumptions would be required to argue for a flying saucer and an alien being.

Is the proof as great as the claim?

A Canadian woman sometimes exhibited the crucifixion wounds of Jesus—allegedly produced supernaturally. In 2002, I watched blood stream from her hands and feet and from tiny scalp wounds like those from a crown of thorns.

However, because her wounds were already bleeding, they could have been self-inflicted. The lance wound that pierced Jesus' side was absent, and the supposed nail wounds did not pass through the hands and feet, being only on one side of each. Getting a closer look, I saw that one hand wound was only a small slit, not a large puncture wound. Therefore, this extraordinary claim lacked the extraordinary proof required.

These three questions should prove helpful in approaching claims and tales in Freaky Phenomena. I view the progress of science as a continuing series of solved mysteries. Perhaps you too might consider a career as a science detective. You can get started right here.

Joe Nickell
Senior Research Fellow, Committee for Skeptical Inquiry
Amherst, NY

MIND OVER MATTER

The relationship between mind, body, and the external world is a complicated one that has fascinated philosophers, scientists, and spiritual seekers for centuries. Do our thoughts impact reality? Can we will certain situations into being? What are the limits of human consciousness?

A popular saying of Zen Buddhism is "mind over matter." It means, essentially, that the force of the human will is powerful enough to overcome physical challenges. Some people use this phrase to help them get through life's daily difficulties, such as a tough workout, a bout of afternoon fatigue, or even an awkward social situation. You might say the words are a way of "psyching" yourself up to be strong in the face of adversity. But there are those who go further than just positive thinking. They believe we can directly affect the physical world—or even transport ourselves outside it—using our minds alone.

In this volume, we'll take an up-close look at some of these psychic phenomena. We'll meet a French girl who was believed to be able to move furniture with her mind, and a young man from Michigan said to be able to start fires with his breath alone. We'll examine the similarities and differences between telepathy and clairvoyance (two supposed methods of mental communication) and check out some claims from history—like the nineteenth-century "thought reader" who died a mysterious death and the Maori boy from New Zealand who apparently used extrasensory abilities to locate long-buried sacred stones. Finally, we'll travel to the "astral plane," where believers are thought to leave their bodies behind to interact with the spiritual world.

We are still unraveling the mysteries of the human mind. And like any unsolved mystery, it is important to maintain a critical eye while examining the evidence. Even scientists acknowledge the limits of human knowledge in comprehending an infinite universe. But as the sphere of our understanding continues to expand, we may discover new dimensions of human beings. Perhaps things that seem inexplicable or outlandish today will be accounted for tomorrow. In the meantime, claims of psychic abilities invite us to keep our analytical skills sharp without losing our natural curiosity. The stories explored here should help you strike that balance.

The third eye in some spiritual traditions, such as Hinduism, symbolizes the gateway to higher consciousness. It is also often associated with psychic phenomena, including clairvoyance and out-of-body experience.

CHAPTER 1

PSYCHOKINESIS

This trick photograph makes it look as though the man is making the wine glass float in midair.

At the end of the 1979 film *Stalker* by Russian filmmaker Andrei Tarkovsky, a young girl named Monkey stares down the length of a table on which three glasses are placed. One by one the glasses move toward the edge of the table. The last falls to the floor. There are no visible wires, strings, or other mechanisms that would help propel the glasses; it seems that Monkey has used only the power of her mind.

The scene depicts the phenomenon of **psychokinesis**, also known as **telekinesis** or PK: the ability to move physical objects using mind power alone. While the example above comes from a science fiction film, there are some people who attest that this phenomenon is real. A 2006 survey by Baylor University found that over 28 percent of participants believed in the possibility of telekinesis.

Skeptical Science

Although researchers have done tests to see if telekinesis is real, there is very little scientific evidence to support it. In the 1930s and '40s, a scientist from Duke University named J. B. Rhine conducted a series of experiments to see whether subjects could influence the outcomes and positions of rolled dice by their minds alone. At first his findings seemed to suggest a correlation between the workings of human consciousness and physical matter, but other researchers had difficulty replicating his exper-

Words to Understand

Exorcise: To expel an evil spirit from a person or place.

Psychokinesis: The ability to move or manipulate objects using the mind alone.

Séance: A gathering where people try to establish contact with the dead.

Spiritualism: A religious movement that believes the spirits of the dead can communicate with the living.

Telekinesis: Another term for psychokinesis. The ability to move or manipulate objects using the mind alone.

iments. Later studies with dice suggested that subjects were altering their behaviors to fit with preconceived beliefs, a tendency known as *confirmation bias*.

A 2014 study from the University of London demonstrated how the power of suggestion can influence people's beliefs. Subjects in the experiment were shown a video of a psychic supposedly bending a metal key with only his mind. He then placed the key on a table and asserted it would continue to bend. If a "co-witness" who was in on the experiment suggested that the key continued to bend, the subject was more likely to believe it did too.

Despite inconclusive scientific backing, those who maintain a belief in telekinesis say that the human brain is actually stronger than we think, and that some people can tap hidden reserves of brainpower to influence the physical world. Others claim that the electrical currents of brainwaves themselves can act on objects. Scientists have debunked both of these beliefs. We do not use merely 10 percent of our brain, as is often reported; almost all of it is active throughout the waking day. And brainwaves are too weak to travel far enough beyond the skull to move matter.

In 19th-century France, the "Electric Girl" was alleged to have had telekinetic powers.

The "Electric Girl"

People throughout history have claimed to have telekinetic powers. One of the most famous is from the 19th century—the "Electric Girl," Angelique Cottin. She hailed from the provincial town of La Perriere in the Normandy region of France, and her powers began to surface around 1846. While she was weaving gloves on a wooden frame, the frame began to shake, apparently of its own power. Heavy pieces of furniture such as chairs, beds, and tables would skitter across the room when she came near them. Other people who came into contact with her reported getting electric shocks.

Cottin's parents took her to a local priest to be **exorcised**, but the priest had her sent to a doctor instead. The doctor was convinced of her powers and called a physicist friend to confirm his impressions. The physicist set up a committee to determine whether the girl's condition was real. Though they observed only one example—a chair shaking when she sat in it—it was enough for the committee; they published a report in the pages of a scientific journal that Cottin's power was legitimate.

Cottin's abilities reportedly ceased in April 1846, though this may have been a way for her to avoid further tests with the committee. Nonetheless, her parents persisted in exhibiting her

Learn more about the girl with electric powers.

Séances are gatherings where people try to communicate with the dead.

For a Séance in the Dark

In the 19th century, telekinesis was associated with **Spiritualism**, a religious movement that believed in the communication between the dead and the living. Spiritualist mediums—people who could supposedly "channel" the voices of the dead—claimed they could move, levitate, or otherwise disrupt objects in a room during **séances**.

Eusapia Palladino was an Italian medium who was reported to have levitated tables and made musical instruments play by themselves. Her powers were widely investigated during her visits to England, America, France, and Germany. While she managed to convince some people, others caught her using trickery—such as lifting a table with her foot to make it appear like it was floating—a few too many times. Today she is widely regarded as a very clever illusionist.

The illusionist and professed psychic Uri Geller became famous for tricks such as bending spoons seemingly with his mind.

to paying customers. Whether she was a master illusionist or did have, as the committee believed, some sort of electromagnetic power remains a mystery lost to time.

Spoonman

Closer to our time, the Israeli illusionist and professed psychic Uri Geller is well known for his telekinetic abilities. He began his career in the 1970s and soon became one of the world's most popular entertainers. In televised performances and live shows all over the globe, he bent spoons and altered the speed of watches seemingly using only his mind. The U.S. Central Intelligence Agency even recruited Geller to aid in their operations, testing to see if he could mentally trigger an atomic bomb.

Geller's abilities have long been questioned by skeptics, however, including other magicians. They claim that his spoon-bending abilities are not the product of psychic powers but are rooted in basic magic tricks. A 1982 book by magician James Randi, *The Truth About Uri Geller,* attempted to disprove many of Geller's trademark psychic feats.

In 1991, Geller sued Randi for slander to the tune of $15 million, but the case was dismissed four years later. Geller was ordered to pay a settlement of $120,000 for filing a "frivolous" lawsuit.

CHAPTER 2

PYROKINESIS

Pyrokinesis is the supposed ability to ignite fires simply by imagining them.

Pyrokinesis is the supposed psychic ability to stop and start fires using the mind alone. The term is derived from two Greek words: *pyro*, meaning "fire," and kinesis, meaning "movement." It was coined by horror novelist Stephen King in his 1980 book *Firestarter*, which features a young girl named Charlie who is able to ignite fires simply by imagining them.

At various points in history there have been people who have claimed pyrokinetic abilities. Some said they could change their internal temperature as well as the temperature of the surrounding atmosphere. Other pyrokinetic practitioners were said to be able to generate fire using their breath or handle blazing objects like lumps of coal with their bare hands. Such claims have been met with skepticism throughout the ages.

On the Atomic Level

Psychokinesis is related to the phenomenon of telekinesis. If telekinesis is the ability to move entire objects with the mind, psychokinesis—according to people who try to explain it—is the ability to move the tiny particles called **atoms** that make up an object.

All matter is made up of atoms. Within each atom are three particles: protons, electrons, and neutrons. Atoms can bond by sharing electrons, forming **molecules**. Atoms and molecules join together to create solids, liquids, and gases. The difference between each of these states is the way in which the atoms are structured: in solids, they are locked tightly in place; in liquids, they move a bit more freely

Words to Understand

Atom: The smallest, most basic unit of matter.

Combustible: An object capable of catching fire easily.

Molecule: A group of two or more atoms bonded together.

Although there is no scientific evidence for pyrokinesis, it would be a fun superpower to have.

but still retain the shape of the container they're held in; and in gases, they careen all over with lots of space between them. All this atomic motion produces the energy we know as heat. The more vigorously the atoms move, the more heat is generated.

Those who believe in pyrokinesis say that some people can mentally speed up atoms to create heat. If the object on which they are focusing their attention is **combustible** they can allegedly vibrate its atoms so vigorously that it bursts into flames. Other believers theorize that

there is a subatomic particle called a *pyrotron* that traverses through the atoms of the human body; when it makes contact with a certain part of the atom called a quark, the theory states, it causes a combustible reaction.

There are all sorts of explanations for this phenomenon, from the skeptically scientific to the more mystically minded. On the mystical end of the spectrum, one self-proclaimed authority on spontaneous combustion, Larry Arnold, has offered the theory of *kundalini*—an

Some have tried to explain pyrokinesis as moving atoms with your mind.

energy source believed by some Eastern religions to be found at the base of the spine. When one's kundalini gets out of whack, it is believed to impact the body physically, including by raising its temperature.

Other theories of spontaneous combustion include an excess of static electricity in the body, a buildup of alcohol or methane, or even "geophysical energy" trapped underneath the earth.

Scientists remain highly doubtful of these explanations, and of spontaneous human combustion in general. The closest thing to a theory of spontaneous combustion science has offered is the "wick effect." This is when a person's body is touched by an external fire source such as a cigarette. Melting fat seeps into the clothing and acts like the wax of a candle, allowing the "wick" of the clothing to continue to burn. The theory may explain why victims' surroundings are often unharmed while their bodies are badly burned.

Watch scenes from the movie based on Stephen King's *Firestarter*.

Pyrokinesis in Paw Paw . . .

In 1882, a young African American man named A.W. Underwood was reported to have pyrokinetic powers. Underwood hailed from Paw Paw, MI, and was well known for being able to start fires using only his breath. Townsfolk said that the intensity of the fire was unpredictable, and so he had to be careful of where and how he breathed.

Underwood went to a local doctor, L.C. Woodman, and told him of his ability. The doctor was skeptical but agreed to run scientific tests on the young man. With several of Woodman's colleagues in attendance, Underwood performed his fire-breathing feats. The doctor was amazed and proclaimed the phenomenon legit. He wrote a report to the local *Michigan Medical News* stating that he had subjected Underwood "to the most rigid examination"—including washing out his mouth and forcing him to wear special gloves—but could find no evidence of a hoax.

Investigations continued, and Underwood even became the subject of an article in *Scientific American*. Skeptics, however, point to the way that Underwood would blow on a handkerchief while rubbing it in his hands before it miraculously ignited. They say he was hiding a piece of phosphorous in his mouth, which he would spit out into the handkerchief. The heat generated by his breath and the friction caused the phosphorous to combust.

Spontaneous Human Combustion

The idea of a pyrotron has been used to explain another phenomenon related to pyrokinesis, that of spontaneous human combustion. This is when a person's body suddenly catches fire, seemingly without being touched by an outside heat source. Cases of spontaneous combustion have been reported for centuries. Victims tend to have a few characteristics in common: although the bulk of the body may be charred, the extremities are often untouched; there is usually a pungent residue of grease, ash, and smoke; and the objects surrounding the person remain intact.

Cases of spontaneous human combustion have been reported for centuries though there is no real evidence to support the phenomenon.

. . . and in the Philippines

In 2011, a three-year-old girl in Antique Province, Philippines, drew headlines for her supposed ability to predict the occurrence of fires. The girl's parents told stories of how she saw a flaming tricycle tire in advance, and how she casually remarked one day, "Something will burn"—only to have a shirt on a nearby clothesline go up in flames within seconds. Whether this was mere co-incidence, an elaborate hoax, or something else entirely, local authorities were alarmed enough to secure the family's home.

CHAPTER 3

TELEPATHY

Telepathy is the supposed ability of people to communicate using only their minds.

I n 2014, scientists rigged up an elaborate system that enabled a person in India to communicate the words *hola* and *ciao* (Spanish and Italian, respectively, for "hello") to three different people in France. In this age of instantaneous communication like texts and emails, that sounds pretty routine. But here's the catch: the sender didn't type or speak these words, but "beamed" them from their brain to the brains of their recipients. This made the event one of the first "brain-to-brain" exchanges on record. The researchers want to continue to improve this technology so that, one day, we may be able to communicate with each other using only our minds. Scientists believe such innovations could help people who cannot speak to interact with others.

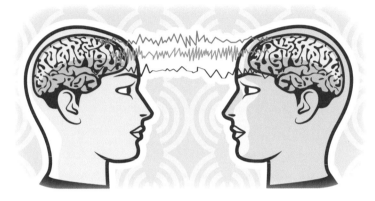

Telepathic communication would involve "beaming" thoughts without speaking.

Words to Understand

Paranormal: Beyond the realm of the normal; outside of commonplace scientific understanding.

Pseudoscience: Beliefs or practices that may appear scientific, but have not been proven by any scientific method.

Subconscious: The part of the mind that we are not aware of but that influences our thoughts, feelings, and behaviors.

Telepathy: Communication between people using the mind alone and none of the five senses.

Scientists can measure the electrical currents in the brain using electroencephalography, or EEG.

The Science of Telepathy

Because the experiment above required the physical apparatus of computers, sensors, and special headsets to stimulate the nerve cells in the recipients' brains, scientists maintain that it was not an example of **telepathy**. The truth is, there is scant scientific evidence for the phenomenon of telepathy, and the concept itself is often dismissed as **pseudoscience** by experts. Although researchers may one day find a way to remove the computers and sensors and enable direct mental communication, such breakthroughs are a long way off.

What is true is that our brain cells communicate with each other by sending chemical messengers across the gaps between cells. This results in tiny sparks of electricity. All of this electrochemical activity produces brainwaves, which vary in intensity depending on what activity we are engaged in; this ranges from high-frequency beta waves when we are most alert to extremely low-frequency delta waves when we are in a deep, dreamless sleep. Scientists can measure these brainwaves with a method known as *electroencephalography*, or EEG. Though the electrical currents in the brain can be recorded and artificially stimulated, they are not powerful enough to radiate information like radio signals.

Other attempts to explain telepathy include the psychological idea that our subconscious mind has the as-yet-unproven power to perceive thought on a deeper, interpersonal level. Another attempted explanation is that certain parts of our brains can send and receive "vibrations" that communicate information in a nonverbal way, such as through shared emotions or perceived images. None of these hypotheses have been tested or proven in any way, however, and for now telepathy remains more science fiction than actual science.

Examining the Evidence

Limited scientific backing hasn't stopped people from examining—or claiming—telepathic abilities. The word *telepathy* was coined in 1882 by Frederic W. H. Myers, a poet, scholar, and investigator into all things **paranormal**. A group he founded, the Society for Psychical Research, investigated

In a 2008 study, scientists used magnetic resonance imaging (MRI) to try to identify the parts of the brain activated during supposed telepathy.

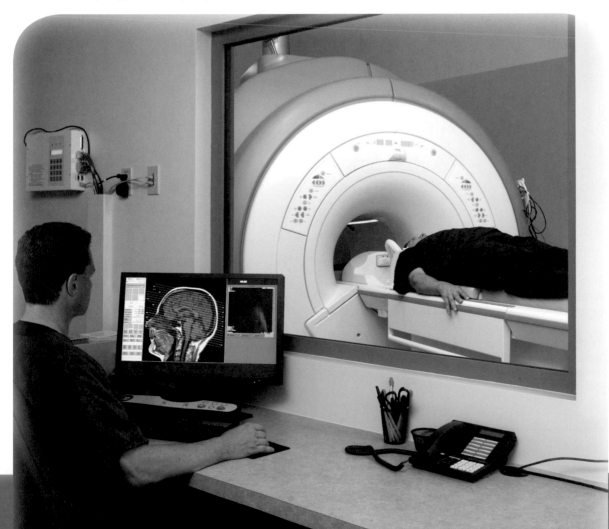

Mind reading, similar to telepathy, has long been a popular entertainment.

Experiments test whether telepathy is real.

telepathy, apparitions, and other strange phenomena; the society published its findings in such books as the 1886 two-volume *Phantasms of the Living.* The group's work was criticized by the scientific community, however, which claimed that the cases featured in the volumes read more like stories than controlled, analyzed scientific experiments.

In 2008, a study in the *International Journal of Yoga* examined the relationship between telepathy and the brain. The study featured two participants: one with a self-avowed telepathic ability, known as a "mentalist," and another who claimed no such skill. Both subjects were placed in magnetic resonance imaging (MRI) machines to measure their brain activity. When the mentalist was engaged in a supposed telepathic task, specific parts of his brain associated with the limbic system—involved in processing our emotions and memories, among other things—were activated. The other participant's brain was activated in a completely different place. From these findings researchers proposed that there may be a connection between telepathic activity and certain regions of the brain.

The Bizarre Death of a Mentalist

Washington Irving Bishop was a 19th-century mentalist who performed acts of "thought reading," similar in nature to telepathy. A main part of Bishop's act was to ask an audience member to hide an object somewhere in the theater. He would then hold the wrist of the volunteer, command them to visualize the location, and—as if by magic—seek out the hidden object. The performance was enhanced by his distinctively dramatic movements, brought on by bouts with catalepsy—a trance-like state where the body becomes suddenly rigid.

Though his act was a memorable one, it wasn't rooted in psychic ability but rather the technique of muscle reading. Bishop himself acknowledged this, saying that his true skill lay in detecting the thoughts of his volunteers by paying careful attention to their unconscious movements.

Perhaps the greatest mystery of Bishop's life wasn't his stage act but the bizarre circumstances of his death. While performing in Manhattan on May 12, 1889, Bishop fell unconscious. He was taken to a nearby bedroom, where he was said to have lapsed into a coma. The following day, believing him dead, doctors performed an autopsy in which they removed his brain. His wife and mother maintained that he had not in fact died, but only suffered a cataleptic fit that left him in a trance-like state; they believed that the doctors had killed him. A second autopsy conducted a few weeks later found his brain sewn inside his chest.

Bishop's mother wrote a book about the ordeal and tried multiple times to take the doctors to court. No one was ever charged. Bishop was buried in Brooklyn's Greenwood Cemetery. His mother had the title "The Martyr" carved into his headstone, an eternal reminder of what she felt was her son's wrongful death.

CHAPTER 4

CLAIRVOYANCE

Fortune tellers often perform with great drama. Their true talent is that they read people very well, figuring out what they want to hear.

lairvoyance comes from the French words for "clear vision." It doesn't relate to powerful eyesight, though, but the ability to see things outside the realm of normal human vision, like details of past or future events or information about people or objects that are far away. Like telepathy, clairvoyance is thought of as a form of **extrasensory perception** (ESP), a mysterious "sixth sense" of the mind.

Early Experiments

Those who believe in the power of clairvoyance generally acknowledge three different manifestations: *precognition* is the ability to glimpse into the future; *retrocognition* is the ability to reconstruct events of the past beyond the range of the clairvoyant's memory; and *remote viewing* is the ability to see events in far-off places as they are happening.

As with most **psychic** phenomena, the scientific opinion on clairvoyance remains decidedly skeptical. Many in the scientific community attribute belief in clairvoyance to "selective thinking," where people only focus on and remember evidence that agrees with their ideas. Skeptics also point to the lack of consistent records of clairvoyance; if it were true, they say, practitioners of clairvoyance would be able to repeat their psychic feats with regularity.

Words to Understand

Ethnologist: A person who studies different cultures, their relationships, and their similarities and differences.

Extrasensory perception: Used to describe perceptive abilities that are not based in the five known senses.

Physiologist: A person who studies the workings of living systems.

Psychic: Of or relating to the mind; often used to describe mental powers that science cannot explain.

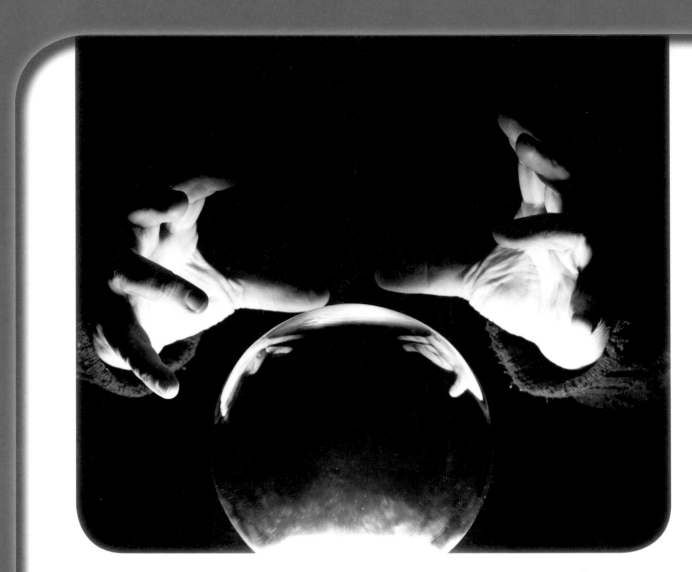

Crystal balls were first used to tell the future 4,000 years ago by the Druids in what is now Britain.

Any lack of compelling evidence has not stopped believers and nonbelievers alike from researching clairvoyance. In the 18th century, the French aristocrat Marquis de Puységar claimed that subjects he hypnotized displayed clairvoyant and telepathic powers. Another Frenchman, the **physiologist** Charles Richet, conducted a similar experiment in 1889 when he hypnotized a woman and had her try to determine the cards inside sealed envelopes. The woman was able to identify some of the cards, but was unable to duplicate her success when Richet repeated the experiment.

Fortune-telling booths are popular at amusement parks.

The Million-Dollar Challenge

Between 1964 and 2015, the James Randi Educational Foundation—named for noted skeptic James Randi (see Chapter 1)—offered a cash prize to anyone who could prove a paranormal ability such as clairvoyance. At the time of the contest's termination in 2015, the prize was up to $1 million. In 2013, the contest featured a contestant who claimed the power of remote viewing. He only managed to identify 3 of 20 objects and so was denied the prize money. The contest drew over a thousand applicants throughout its history. Participants were given the freedom to set the conditions of their demonstrations, but no one ever beat the challenge.

The Search Continues

Cards figured into 20th-century experiments conducted by J.B. Rhine (see Chapter 1) and the psychologist Karl Zener. "Zener cards," as they came to be called, featured five different symbols in a deck of 25 cards. Starting in the 1930s, Zener and Rhine conducted a series of experiments in which they would draw one of the cards, wait for the person being tested for clairvoyance to guess it, and proceed this way through the entire deck. Skeptics of this method say that subjects had opportunities to cheat, such as peering at the cards as they were shuffled. They also claim that the limited amount of potential combinations made it easier to guess the cards.

Today, researchers continue to try to establish a factual basis for clairvoyance. In 2008, former Harvard professor Diane Hennacy Powell published *The ESP Enigma: The Scientific Case for Psychic Phenomena;* among other things, the book examines the psychic experiences of historical figures such as Abraham Lincoln, who is said to have had a dream that foretold his own death. Psychology professor Jeff Zacks of Washington University in Saint Louis has looked into the concept of "predictive perception," or the way we all make predictions throughout the course of

James Randi shows how easy it is to fake psychic powers.

Professional psychics make money off people's desire to believe that they can see the future.

our daily lives. Zacks's research has focused on identifying the parts of the brain where these predictions occur and the processes by which they are made. In addition to helping us understand the science of "everyday clairvoyance," these findings may help people with neurological disorders to regain their decision-making abilities.

Clairvoyance in New Zealand

The search for clairvoyants has extended to the most remote regions of the globe. In 1920, New Zealand **ethnologist** J. Percy Smith published a paper with writer James Cowan about the clairvoyant abilities of the Maori people of New Zealand. The paper described how some Maori could locate long-buried objects, including stones believed to be sacred, by the powers of clairvoyance and hypnosis.

A carving made by the Maori people of New Zealand.

Many of these cases involved Maori elders, but one story focused on the clairvoyant powers of a 17-year-old boy. According to an eyewitness, a group of Maori from Waihi, a town on the north island of New Zealand, were searching for buried stones they felt had the power to attract fish. Maori elders brought the boy to the general area where they thought the stones were buried, though their precise location had been lost to time. They hypnotized the boy while chanting incantations, then set him out to find the stones. After some deliberation, he began digging near an old tree stump. Three feet down he discovered one of the stones, complete with distinctive carvings and a small stone axe.

The boy's clairvoyant exploits didn't end there, however. In 1920, a New Zealand paper published an account of a Maori woman who was skeptical of the boy's abilities and asked him to locate a ring she had lost four years previously. After praying, the boy produced an exact description of the ring and named the road where it was buried. He told the woman that she would need three days to find it. Lo and behold, the woman went to the road and started searching. On the third day, after much discouragement, she found the ring beneath a covering of dirt and grass.

CHAPTER 5

Out-of-Body Experience

The phenomenon of **astral projection**, sometimes referred to as an out-of-body experience, is an ancient one. Traditions of the ancient Egyptians, Hindu scriptures, and Japanese mythology all have stories of this occurrence, and modern spirit seekers like Robert Monroe and V.M. Beelzebub (real name: Mark Pritchard) have kept awareness of the possibility of "consciousness travel" in the public eye.

The word *astral* refers to a plane of existence beyond the **material** world, where, according to some religions and philosophies, spiritual beings such as angels dwell. The soul is thought to pass through the world before birth and after death. In this way the astral plane is sometimes conceived of as a heaven or afterlife, where humans ascend at the end of their physical existence.

Theosophists and other devotees of mystical philosophy speak of an "astral body" that is the physical body's "double." Believers say it provides vital energy to the physical body and connects it with the astral realm. When people experience astral projection, it is the feeling of this astral body departing from the physical one. A widespread theory among devotees of mystical philosophy is that the astral and physical bodies are linked by a "silver thread." This has been interpreted as a type of umbilical cord or a reference to the spine.

Words to Understand

Astral projection: The sensation of the soul, spirit, or consciousness leaving the body; sometimes called an out-of-body experience.

Guru: A spiritual teacher in the Hindu tradition; a person who guides others in philosophical or religious matters.

Involuntary: Not subject to a person's control.

Material: Of or relating to the physical world.

Occult: Of or relating to secret knowledge of supernatural things.

It's All in the Mind

Because there is no scientific proof of the existence of an astral body, soul, or spirit that can transcend the physical world, the scientific community remains skeptical of the premise of astral projection. Even if someone could "leave" his or her body, scientists question the idea that their consciousness would go with them. There is also the problem that few people who say they have experienced astral projection can provide detailed information about their travels.

Claims of astral projection are often dismissed as hallucinations, altered states, or mental disruptions brought on by chemical substances, overactive imaginations, or just plain old wishful thinking.

For these reasons, claims of astral projection are often dismissed as hallucinations, altered states, or mental disruptions brought on by chemical substances, overactive imaginations, or just plain old wishful thinking. One scientific explanation lies in the phenomenon of "near sleep experiences," also known as episodes of "microsleep." During these episodes, a person might fall asleep for a few seconds to a few minutes at a time, often without realizing it. People can even dream during these episodes, causing them to think they have had an extrasensory or paranormal experience upon waking.

Scientists have identified a region of the brain, the temporo-parietal junction (TPJ), that may be related to perceptions of experiences of astral projection. The TPJ is responsible for "tracking" our physical bodies as they move through the world. It situates us in space and keeps us aware of the perimeters of our bodies. Research has shown that disruptions to the workings of the TPJ could cause people to lose a sense of where they are and register what is happening as an out-of-body experience.

Religious Traditions

Many of the world's religious traditions touch on some version of astral projection in their sacred scriptures. The *Mahabharata*, an epic poem composed in the ancient language of Sanskrit and one of the founding documents of India's Hindu culture, contains a description of a main character exiting his physical body. Another Hindu text, the *Yoga Vasistha*, describes the relationship between meditation and transcending one's physical body.

Scientists investigate out-of-body experiences.

Crossing Over

A related type of out-of-body experience is the near-death experience. This is when a person undergoing a life-threatening event, such as an illness or car accident, has the sudden sensation of being "forced" out of their bodies. They may report the sensation of hovering above themselves or even watching doctors attend to their physical bodies. Others claim to see images such as the classic "light at the end of the tunnel," which may represent a passage into the afterlife, or interaction with friends and family members who have long since passed away.

Believers in astral travel describe the difference between astral projection and near-death experiences as one of control: astral projection, they say, can be willed by people through special techniques, whereas a near-death experience is *involuntary*. Furthermore, while in the state of astral projection advanced practitioners are thought to be able to control their movements through the nonphysical realm, directing their astral bodies toward specific destinations.

Seeing a light at the end of a tunnel is a common description of a near-death experience.

Hindu texts describe the relationship between meditation and transcending one's physical body.

Astral projection is believed to be one of the powers, or *siddhis*, of Hindu sages advanced in yogic practice.

In the Christian tradition, a passage in Saint Paul's Second Epistle to the Corinthians appears to describe an out-of-body experience. However, skeptical Christians have questioned whether this was merely a vision, lucid dream, or other more explicable phenomenon.

Madame Blavatsky

In the 19th century, Russian aristocrat-turned-mystic Helen (Madame) Blavatsky made quite a name for herself promoting astral travel, telepathy, and other paranormal powers as within reach of human beings. Blavatsky led a colorful life that included periods of travel to Asia and Europe, and she claimed to have learned spiritual truths directly from Hindu **gurus**.

In 1875, Blavatsky founded the Theosophical Society in New York City with her friend Henry Steel Olcott. Theosophy (from the Greek words for "divine wisdom") is the name for an array of philosophies that seek direct knowledge of the divine; while the term had existed for centuries, it soon became associated with Blavatsky's teachings. Through the Theosophical Society and books such as *Isis Unveiled* and *The Secret Doctrine*, she offered the public a heady mix of mysticism, **occult** notions, and ancient religious concepts. Her work introduced such ideas as reincarnation into mainstream conversation, and for a brief period in the late 19th century theosophy was very popular.

After Blavatsky was accused of fraud and fabricating paranormal events, her influence began to decline. Whether she was a charlatan or a genuine mystic remains a source of debate, though she is often credited with inspiring such modern-day Spiritualist trends as the New Age movement.

Helen (Madame) Blavatsky, the 19th-century Russian aristocrat-turned-mystic.

Series Glossary

Affliction: Something that causes pain or suffering.

Afterlife: Life after death.

Anthropologist: A professional who studies the origin, development, and behavioral aspects of human beings and their societies, especially primitive societies.

Apparition: A ghost or ghostlike image of a person.

Archaeologist: A person who studies human history and prehistory through the excavation of sites and the analysis of artifacts and other physical remains found.

Automaton: A person who acts in a mechanical, machinelike way as if in trance.

Bipolar disorder: A mental condition marked by alternating periods of elation and depression.

Catatonic: To be in a daze or stupor.

Celestial: Relating to the sky or heavens.

Charlatan: A fraud.

Chronic: Continuing for a long time; used to describe an illness or medical condition generally lasting longer than three months.

Clairvoyant: A person who claims to have a supernatural ability to perceive events in the future or beyond normal sensory contact.

Cognition: The mental action or process of acquiring knowledge and understanding through thought, experience, and the senses.

Déjà vu: A sensation of experiencing something that has happened before when experienced for the first time.

Delirium: A disturbed state of mind characterized by confusion, disordered speech, and hallucinations.

Dementia: A chronic mental condition caused by brain disease or injury and characterized by memory disorders, personality changes, and impaired reasoning.

Dissociative: Related to a breakdown of mental function that normally operates smoothly, such as memory and consciousness. Dissociative identity disorder is a mental Trauma: A deeply distressing or disturbing experience.

Divine: Relating to God or a god.

Ecstatic: A person subject to mystical experiences.

Elation: Great happiness.

Electroencephalogram (EEG): A test that measures and records the electrical activity of the brain.

Endorphins: Hormones secreted within the brain and nervous system that trigger a positive feeling in the body.

ESP (extrasensory perception): An ability to communicate or understand outside of normal sensory capability, such as in telepathy and clairvoyance.

Euphoria: An intense state of happiness; elation.

Hallucinate: To experience a perception of something that seems real but is not actually present.

Immortal: Living forever.

Inhibition: A feeling that makes one self-conscious and unable to act in a relaxed and natural way.

Involuntary: Not subject to a person's control.

Karma: A Buddhist belief that whatever one does comes back—a person's actions can determine his or her reincarnation.

Levitate: To rise in the air by supernatural or magical power.

Malevolent: Evil.

Malignant: Likely to grow and spread in a fast and uncontrolled way that can cause death.

Mayhem: Chaos.

Mesmerize: To hold someone's attention so that he or she notices nothing else.

Mindfulness: A meditation practice for bringing one's attention to the internal and external experiences occurring in the present moment.

Monolith: A giant, single upright block of stone, especially as a monument.

Motivational: Designed to promote a willingness to do or achieve something.

Motor functions: Muscle and nerve acts that produce motion. Fine motor functions include writing and tying shoes; gross motor functions are large movements such as walking and kicking.

Mystics: People who have supernatural knowledge or experiences; they have a supposed insight into spirituality and mysteries transcending ordinary human knowledge.

Necromancy: An ability to summon and control things that are dead.

Neurological: Related to the nervous system or neurology (a branch of medicine concerning diseases and disorders of the nervous system).

Neuroplasticity: The ability of the brain to form and reorganize synaptic connections, especially in response to learning or experience, or following injury.

Neuroscientist: One who studies the nervous system

Neurotransmitters: Chemicals released by nerve fibers that transmit signals across a synapse (the gap between nerve cells).

Occult: Of or relating to secret knowledge of supernatural things.

Olfactory: Relating to the sense of smell.

Out-of-body experience: A sensation of being outside one's body, floating above and observing events, often when unconscious or clinically dead.

Papyrus: A material prepared in ancient Egypt from the pithy stem of a water plant, used to make sheets for writing or painting on, rope, sandals, and boats.

Paralysis: An inability to move or act.

Paranoid: Related to a mental condition involving intense anxious or fearful feelings and thoughts often related to persecution, threat, or conspiracy.

Paranormal: Beyond the realm of the normal; outside of commonplace scientific understanding.

Paraphysical: Not part of the physical word; often used in relation to supernatural occurrences.

Parapsychologist: A person who studies paranormal and psychic phenomena.

Parapsychology: Study of paranormal and psychic phenomena considered inexplicable in the world of traditional psychology.

Phobia: Extreme irrational fear.

Physiologist: A person who studies the workings of living systems.

Precognition: Foreknowledge of an event through some sort of ESP.

Premonition: A strong feeling that something is about to happen, especially something unpleasant.

Pseudoscience: Beliefs or practices that may appear scientific, but have not been proven by any scientific method.

Psychiatric: Related to mental illness or its treatment.

Psychic: Of or relating to the mind; often used to describe mental powers that science cannot explain.

Psychokinesis: The ability to move or manipulate objects using the mind alone.

Psychological: Related to the mental and emotional state of a person.

PTSD: Post-traumatic stress disorder is a mental health condition triggered by a terrifying event.

Repository: A place, receptacle, or structure where things are stored.

Resilient: Able to withstand or recover quickly from difficult conditions.

Resonate: To affect or appeal to someone in a personal or emotional way.

Schizophrenia: A severe mental disorder characterized by an abnormal grasp of reality; symptoms can include hallucinations and delusions.

Skeptic: A person who questions or doubts particular things.

Spectral: Ghostly.

Spiritualism: A religious movement that believes the spirits of the dead can communicate with the living.

Stimulus: Something that causes a reaction.

Subconscious: The part of the mind that we are not aware of but that influences our thoughts, feelings, and behaviors.

Sumerians: An ancient civilization/people (5400–1750 BCE) in the region known as Mesopotamia (modern day Iraq and Kuwait).

Synapse: A junction between two nerve cells.

Synthesize: To combine a number of things into a coherent whole.

Telekinesis: Another term for psychokinesis. The ability to move or manipulate objects using the mind alone.

Telepathy: Communication between people using the mind alone and none of the five senses.

Uncanny: Strange or mysterious.

Further Resources

Websites

Theosophical Society in America: *www.theosophical.org/*
The website of the Theosophical Society features information on the history of the theosophical movement, its ideas, and its many publications.

The Rhine: *www.rhine.org/*
Duke University's Rhine Research Center is dedicated to the study of human consciousness, including psychic abilities and other inexplicable phenomena.

Society for Psychical Research: *www.spr.ac.uk/*
This London-based group, founded in 1882, maintains a website with information on research projects, articles, and current events related to paranormal topics.

Movies

Movies often feature paranormal themes. Here are a few you might want to check out.

The Fury
This thriller follows the story of a young boy with psychic powers who is kidnapped by the CIA.

Phenomenon
After being struck by an orb of bright light, an auto mechanic from North Carolina acquires the power of telekinesis in this 1995 movie.

Firestarter
This film adaptation of the Stephen King book by the same name features a young girl with pyrokinetic abilities.

Further Reading

Horn, Stacy. *Unbelievable: Investigations into Ghosts, Poltergeists, Telepathy, and Other Unseen Phenomena, from the Duke Parapsychology Laboratory.* New York: Ecco, 2010.

Jacobson, Annie. *Phenomena: The Secret History of the U.S. Government's Investigations into Extrasensory Perception and Psychokinesis.* New York: Little, Brown and Company, 2017.

Lachman, Gary. *Madame Blavatsky: The Mother of Modern Spirituality.* New York: TarcherPerigee, 2012.

About the Author

Michael Centore is a writer and editor. He has helped produce many titles, including memoirs, cookbooks, and educational materials, for a variety of publishers. He has authored numerous books for Mason Crest, including titles in the Major Nations in a Global World and Drug Addiction and Recovery series. His work has appeared in the Los Angeles Review of Books, Killing the Buddha, Mockingbird, The Clarion Review, and other print- and web-based publications. He lives in Connecticut.

Index